You Can't
Snowman

by Sarah Holliday

ISBN 0-15-314553-6

Ordering Options
ISBN 0-15-314559-5 (Grade K Collection)
ISBN 0-15-314566-8 (package of 5)

Harcourt Brace School Publishers

1 2 3 4 5 6 7 8 9 10 179 2002 2001 2000 99

You can dance.

1

You can sing.

You can swing.

You can jump.

You can run.

You can hide.

You can slide.

You can hug.